GREENHEART

By the same author

In the Hot-house

GREENHEART

ALAN JENKINS

Chatto & Windus

LONDON

For my mother, and for Martin and Krystina Kiersnowski

Published in 1990 by
Chatto & Windus Ltd
20 Vauxhall Bridge Road
London SW1V 2SA

A CIP catalogue record for this book is available from the British Library.
ISBN 0 7011 3646 4

Acknowledgements are due to the editors of the following publications, in which some of these poems first appeared: the *New Statesman*, *Oxford Poetry*, *Pequod*, *Soho Square 1*, the *Sunday Times*, *The Orange Dove of Fiji* (ed. Simon Rae), the *Times Literary Supplement*.

The first poem of the sequence 'The Island Muse' is a translation of 'Isole' by Bartolo Cattafi; another sequence, 'The London Dissector', co-opts one or two phrases from Iain Sinclair's remarkable 'novel', *White Chappell, Scarlet Tracings* (Paladin, 1988).

Photoset in Linotron Ehrhardt by
Rowland Phototypesetting Ltd, Bury St Edmunds, Suffolk
Printed in Great Britain by
Redwood Press Ltd, Melksham, Wiltshire

CONTENTS

Quelle est cette île triste et noire? – C'est Cythère,
Nous dit-on, un pays fameux dans les chansons,
Eldorado banal de tous les vieux garçons.

– Baudelaire, Un Voyage à Cythère

. . . I must be silent, these are dangerous times to libel a
man in, much more a world.

– John Keats, to Georgina

I rarely heard a sound in that forest, though there was a bird
which called. I often heard it in the woods of the upper
Madeira. It called thrice, as a boy who whistles shrilly
through his fingers; a long call, and then another whistle in
the same key followed instantly by a falling note.

– H. M. Tomlinson, The Sea and the Jungle

Heat

So this was the Isle of Pines – half-way
through Co. Kerry . . . The Isle of Pines!
It flares up in the mind
like a matchflame, and is gone.

We chafe each other for the hot, wet spark
and, now, land-masses melting, glaciers melting –
watched by satellite, miles above our heads . . .
Then wake up dead in our beds.

An archaeologist or hunter-gatherer, the first
to emerge from primeval forest
is led by what's left of his nose
to a strangely glittering black barrow:

sheets of polythene held down by row
on row of tyres. Unnatural quiet. Unnatural dark.
Inside, a litter of bones, bottles, tins; a few
cyanide capsules in a box marked SHELTER.

*

A thousand million tiny fish
in a flap, helpless on the sheet –
which one will dare
the path between the barbed-wire fence

and the wall of heat?
(On one side, women stare
at blank eyes. Blank eyes stare back.
A Sad Sack

guard
will whip out his own Cruise
and demonstrate its use.
It is already hard.

Night and day,
a welter of woodsmoke, mud; the tents
of sticks and stones and black plastic rubbish-
bags; the darkening silos.)

*

I cycled five miles through potato-fields and forest,
past the Deer Haven, Canine Country Club
and Lobster Claw. The hub
of the bicycle I'd borrowed

clicked and whined; she was behind, on an older model,
struggling a little. Half-way between the home of Robert Frost
and that of Robert Penn Warren, I walked in through maple
and spruce-pine, and, with her beside me, rowed

my son across the moonlit lake. Hers,
by the wide brown eyes. The jagged silhouettes of firs,
the denser mass of mountain peaks. He bent close to tell me
that every river in Vermont was dry – the dripping oar,

his small voice the only sounds; we could see two hayricks
burning, cars in laybys burning. I struck out for the shore.
While she and I lay down among the melting rocks
he would water his one bare tree.

Isaac

It hurt me, the hand that pinned my neck,
my cheek. I cried out as the knife came nearer –
he wanted it close enough to nick
my nose or ear if I struggled. A quick sob of terror –
The mystery, he said, *of fathers, sons,*
of faith as strong as love, as all our sins –
he spoke in riddles sometimes. He taught me Wilfred Owen:
Half the seed of Europe, one by one . . .

I shared his bed of straw and sackcloth,
carried jars of wine, cooked little fish
and brought him apples, figs and apricots on a copper dish;
I watched him eat and drink in silence
or busied myself with the backcloth,
the pigments, clothes for the Virgin and soldiers.
As the young god, I bared my shoulders
and daintily held out a glass,
my face suffused with the various glows
that wine, or he, had leant its pallor –
the invitation not unambiguous.

He froze me leaping to escape the violence
that was done to Matthew –
the sword raised, the old man cowering, the intriguers
skulking nearby; in that instant,
in Abyssinia, of his becoming a saint
(I understood later – at the time I was a glance-puller
with my ear-ring and a well-placed tattoo)
everyone looks into, or away from, the abyss.

Album

The wall of little windows, mirrors that show her
in sun-raked rooms, naked from bed, bath or shower
(she has become their martyr),
washstand, soap and jug, the surprising pestle and mortar,
the mirror that sees nothing of all this . . .
You step into *La Chambre Turque* by Balthus,
a child who holds a glass that never shatters,
or out to the balcony in Bonnard's *Window with Green*
                                                            Shutters.

Offerings

High above Paris, the three 'book-lined rooms'
he offered us to flop in between museums
had a museum quality of their own:
the *White Cup and Saucer* by Fantin-Latour
(still the still point, all this time later,
of a blustery Cambridge afternoon
– though on the reverse of this card, an offer
of love, tentative, unconditional, too late or too soon);
a vase of tulips, blowsy, overblown
(so unlike the tulips I once sent in lieu
of other offers, that would never open up
for anyone, that, until they died, had stood
in a vase in the room I'd left, by then, for good . . .)
Finally the Alto Rhapsody she'd wanted me to hear
(I played it to extinction, thinking of her).
She pounced on it, and after a while I pounced too,
pressed her down hard against the sofa
with its covering of rugs from Turkestan,
gripped her shoulders – then my cup
was running over, then sadness, a little stain . . .

Sofa

In a layby just outside Southampton, L.I.,
a four-seater beige plush sofa
sat under trees, as if for some shade and a rest,
as if it had put down roots. Who had laid it by?

Heavy petting under the constellations,
her chewing-gum swallowed, his hand on her breast,
the radio playing in a parked Studebaker
and the moon silvering a field of rutabaga . . .

Someone had wanted it to suffer
the indignity of exposure – rips and stains
down all its velvet-covered length, its fringe;
bums who stopped to sleep on it (but there are no bums

on Long Island), and pissed themselves, or worse –
and this had been the perfect revenge
on the hated in-laws, whose wedding-gift
it was, way back. A casualty of wars

too old and awful for words, the alcohol-wars,
wife-wars, the skirmishes of mobile homes,
it had featured in a nightmare of repossession,
had a story to tell, a sad one, of continental drift.

Phaeacian

She'd watched, on and off, all day
the windsurfers slicing cleanly back
and forth across the bay,
clinging to their wishbones. She'd kept track

of that one who almost fell
but pulled himself up every time.
Then when she'd had her fill
she began the long climb

to the bar, the table under pines,
the unstable view of the sea
and a glass or two of retsina.
Alone was how she liked to be

and how she most often was –
the local boys had tried their luck
but she'd never taken to their streetwise
cruelty, their macho fear, their central lack.

This one was different – he always is.
When he came in, carrying his board,
grinning, she met his sea-blue eyes,
saw the salt drying in his beard.

He was the one she'd watched. He sat down. Then, she had
no idea why it came into her head,
she asked him back to her father's homestead.
Five miles inland. They took her moped.

Her name was Nausicaä,
she worked as a chambermaid
in a local pension – it drove her mad
so she would slip away

and spend every minute
that she could, by the sea or in it.
He was called Odysseus, a second mate
on a tanker – small chance that they would meet . . .

On the way, she stopped to swell a creek.
Crickets sang in chorus,
in their ancient Greek,
a *skiouros*

cocked its tail-fur
at the sight of her.
From the road he caught a glimpse
of a dark isosceles, and lumps

throbbed in his throat and jeans.
Her father's house was single-storey, small;
a vine-strung trellis, rows of tomatoes, beans,
a goat tethered to an outhouse wall.

She went inside. A lamp was lit. Moths flew.
Some words he could not hear.
He watched the doorway where she would appear
to beckon him in, wondered how he knew.

Broken Shutter

The edge of light. The very edge.
The palpable darkness, out of which
you will see emerge
a Grecian urn.

She is herself the heroine
of a story she will sketch
around its base:
'The secretary and her boss',

'What the blacksmith saw' . . . Snakes and lizards
scatter at the shutter's unhinged screech;
Pandora's creaking door

gives on a room, a box of brushes, paints,
on the fire-hazard
of her hair, and,
when she turns, the points

of her breasts, that urge
on you the palpable darkness in which
you can discern
the edge of light, the very edge.

Kombitsi

Pine-cones on the roof outside the window
and littering the fern-shadowed path,
the smarting from each pine-cone
turned to smoke.
                              Dew-drench.
The room like a Turkish bath,
a mildew-map on the ceiling, mildew-stench.

The scorpion as it scuttles from the stone,
the lizard blinking in its hexagon of sun.

The tattered pages of *Swann's Way*
ranged on the windowsill alongside M. M. Kaye.

The pink neoclassical façade
of the watering-place
where sheep and goats may safely graze,
its fresco of lichen, its dripping green shade.

The mirror painted with L O V E
in the psychedelic years. A frazzled wasp.

Olive-leaves shimmying to the slightest breeze,
a donkey groaning under its hump of straw.
A moped leaning on a wall of heat.

A jangle of wire nerves behind the door,
the water-pipes' asthmatic wheeze,
the clack and rasp
of shutters thrown back on themselves.

A grinning peasant-Prospero calling for Miranda
from the orange or the lemon grove.

Cockroach-husks, mosquito-ghosts on shelves.
The umpteenth glass. The umpteenth card.

The black bee as big as a clenched fist,
fireflies winking and flashing the way home
to a bare room,
a wide brass bed, a damp white sheet.

Rain in the pine-forest. Love-in-a-mist.

Rain in the Pine-Forest
(from D'Annunzio)

Hush. The edge
of the forest. I can't hear
those human words
you're saying,
only the language
of distant
rain-drops and leafage.
Listen.
It's raining from the strung-out
clouds. It's raining
on the tamarisks,
salty, parched;
on the scaly,
bristling pines,
on the sacred
myrtle,
on the broom that flames
with clusters of flowers,
on the junipers,
thickly-hung
with scented berries,
raining
on our leaf-surrounded faces,
on our bare hands,
our flimsy

clothes, on our two minds,
freshened, still thirsting;
on the beautiful fiction
which yesterday
seduced you, which
today seduces me,
my lover.

Do you hear? The rain falls
on this abandoned
forest-growth
with a rustling
that comes and goes,
deepens, fades on the air
as the leaves are more or less
scarce.
Listen. Only
the cicada's song
replies to the sound of weeping, a song
that neither
the murmured lamentation of the south
nor the ashen sky
appals.
And the pine makes one sound,
the myrtle another, the juniper
yet another,
each one an instrument
played by innumerable fingers,
and we
are wholly immersed
in the spirit of the forest,
we are alive with the trees' life,
and your intoxicated features
are rain-softened like a leaf,
your hair has the scent
of the glowing broom,
earthly creature
whom

I call
my lover.

Listen, listen. Those airy nothings the cicadas
are drowned out little by little,
but a hoarser song
rises from the remote
dank shadows –
the one note
that trembles, fades,
rises, trembles, fades.
We cannot hear
the sea's voice,
or anything but the splash and hiss
of drenching, purifying, silver rain,
a noise of metal being beaten –
louder, fainter, as
the leaves are more or less
close.
The frog, daughter of the distant marshlands,
is singing from shadowy dark somewhere,
and the rain falls on your eyelashes –
it's as if you wept,
but with pleasure –
as green-white you emerge
like a dryad from the bark.
We twine and part,
twine and part, like thickets,
their greenness fetters and ensnares us,
it's raining on our sylvan faces,
our hands, our flimsy
clothes, our freshened souls,
on the beautiful fiction which yesterday
seduced me, today
seduces you, my lover.

Babes

At 2 or 3 a.m.
I left the discothèque,
stumbling after her
down half a mountainside,

waving away
the pine-needle cobwebs
from my face,
following

her torch's flickering light
on the path
strewn with rocks
like stepping-stones

in a fast-flowing
pine-needle river
into which I might slip
and lose myself for ever . . .

A palisade
staked out with pine.
Still I followed,
despite

the hot breath of two waist-high
German sheepdogs
on my neck.
Then the hut built of that same stone,

the pile of logs,
the hearth
that filled a whole room
and the bed of blankets and fur.

Her two children asleep
upstairs, we two, four
babes
in the wood.

The Island Muse

Calliope

Your islands show
little
by little rising
over the horizon
or coming clear
at a stroke,
the hard-edged profile,
the archipelago
your territories open to the sun
and to the mist
founded on nothing
fearful of a breath
how much life already behind
what a sea already crossed

Clio

A sea already crossed, my great-great-great grandfather
was valet, so the story goes,
to the great Napoleon on Elba,
and brought him, every morning at first light
as he stood in his nightshirt like an alb,
coffee, bread, olives and a breast of goose.

That's his goose cooked. I see them, shy and awkward
and at a loss, unable to get much further
than some droll asides on perfidious Albion,
my great-great-great grandfather thinking of an orchard
in Wicklow, and the great Napoleon
musing, not on his imperial palace,
amaranths and palms, but goats in scrub and heather,
a mad dog loping round a dusty *place*.

Erato

Round a dusty *place*, old men, stubbly, gap-toothed,
sat in the shade and pondered the explosion – bomb,
gun-shot, or the twice-daily bus
backfiring on the hill. Neither they nor their daughters,
surly and dark-eyed in the grain-scattered yard
among washing and a flurry of hens,
seemed to like what was between us
as we struggled down a steep path towards the water,
the beach (lunar, black pebbles, scorching, smooth),
through a tunnel of bees – booming, buzzing greenness,
a honeysuckle-arch among the vines.
Perhaps it was our glaring white goose-flesh (we swam
naked, and they watched); perhaps my getting hard
as we lay, half-dozing to a far-off, drowsy hum.

Euterpe

Half-dozing to a far-off drowsy hum
of reggae, air-conditioners and fans
he lies and smokes, and sweats, and thinks of home,
the village near Kilmarnock, and his plans
to renovate this place – six bamboo huts
round a pool, a fly-blown dining-room and bar.
He can't get the staff – the German (Christ, how he hates
that bastard!) is only good for swilling beer
and poking chambermaids, or, if he's lucky, guests:
in their forties, American, divorced . . .

He wonders what to make of the English pair
in Five, the guy an 'intellectual', half-arsed
colonial crap, show-off, boogie-lover, poor;
the girl each night to a steel band swaying her lovely breasts.

Polyhymnia

Swaying, her lovely breasts catch the sun-glint
as the bus rocks at speed from side to side of the road.
Sheer drop one side; on the other, terraced mountain.
The bus is full of black boots, caps; someone has eaten,
for lunch, a whole raw pig and a string of onions.
The woman on the seat in front of us is being sick
into a paper bag, which proves unequal to her noisome vomit.

But the radio is turned up full-blast, and from it
pours a never-ceasing, never-changing stream of music
and song, high-pitched, agonised, like a man walking on his
                                          bunions
or a donkey being repeatedly, mercilessly beaten;
our knowledgeable companion informs us that this fountain
has its source in the joy of one who, exiled, has greatly sorrowed,
who returns to his village, his mother, to die, wasted, skint.

Melpomene

To die, wasted, skint, in the middle of an ocean,
in the middle of nowhere, a rock best left to wind and sheep;
to get your stomach churned up by a heaving snot-green sea
and then to get fried in a floating chip-shop
(which chip was you?), a meal for fishes at the bottom;
to get your meat-and-two-veg cut off in some bushes
and stuffed in your mouth, because you're keen on 'revolution',
i.e. *not* keen on curfews, death-squads and a GNP
that the colonel's mistress spends when she's shopping for shoes;
to be shipped off your home on an atoll (next to *atom*
in the dictionary) that will give its name – meaning things in
                                          twos –
to the skimpy rags that don't cover tits and bums on beaches,
that, when they've finished with it, when the last jetstream
has faded, is strange growths, flotsam and jetsam.

Terpsichore

'Flotsam and jetsam', the local author calls these lads;
couriers, tour-operators call them 'shithouses',
pack them into half-built hangars on sewage-swamped
                                                    seafronts –
a scorched strip of tarmac, supermarkets, neon bars;
twin beds and balconies from which (having kicked off
hours before on lager, got through carafe after carafe
of the local red and nine of barman Taki's specials,
then the last drops of duty-free Chartreuse)
they puke extravagantly; piss; shoot their loads –
shouting *Stavros is a wanker* at the stars.

Tonight they fling plates in the vine-roofed taverna, linking
arms for their Zorba-dance, yelling *Arsenal are cunts*;
later, in a brawl over a girl, they'll break up the disco,
leave blood, shattered glass, crazed strobe-lights still blinking.

Urania

Lights still blinking from the shore-
shaped smudge of black; the ferry
judders through a diesel-haunted surge, ploughs its furrow
in wind and water, salty noise; on the bridge,
gale warnings out of Roscoff, Brest, the Faroes . . .

Was it written in the stars that the Bay of Biscay
would find new latitudes? Dover to Calais, Fishguard
to Rosslare, I gravitate towards the aristocracy
that sired in straw –
backwards, I mean, to great-grandmother Louise Fitzgerald,
shy looks, apple cheeks, shipped to England and marriage
in 1890 – but cannot name the heavenly bodies or find the
                                                    pole star
as I once could, or remember how to steer
my way in whatever is taking its course.

Thalia

Whatever is taking its course, it seems as if –
a sea already crossed – I shall always be
a boat adrift, or a mad dog loping round a dusty place,
my place, coming back for comfort to the island of a desk
to dream of lying in a hammock slung on deck,
cradling an ocarina, dozing to a far-off
drowsy hum made by the engines, in front of me
a dark-skinned girl uncurling, bending over forwards to please,
swaying her lovely breasts in moonlight, crooning in her soft
                                                    voice
a song of the Fortunate Isles, where we are headed,
where I shall set up camp, cultivate every vice –
only to die, wasted, skint (the boy already dead),
among grinning faces, flotsam and jetsam; on a farther shore
lights still blinking; sad and dark, now, your islands show.

Reins

She still has them somewhere, she tells me,
the harness with its three blue bears,
the cream-coloured reins she tied to a rail
while, strapped in at the other end,
I toddled round the deck of her daddy's boat –
sea-weed and salt, gull-cry, wave-slap.

She feels them slipping through her fingers,
then a tug, I've fallen flat on my face
but I'm up and beaming into father's Rollei:
little sailor-boy, quilted, kitted out
with life-jacket, harness, reins that trail
past stanchions, hatches, cleats; she takes up the slack . . .

Her father dead, my father's had his first attack.
They've slipped through her fingers some more
and she's giving me free rein in her own house
to come in at all hours, drunk, or with a friend,
and leave my trophy (a pair of tide-marked tights) in my drawer
among the letters in a rounded, girlish hand:
                    *
I was getting kitted out for life,
or so I thought (though when she showed the snap
to someone new, I squirmed; in harness, reined –
was that how she saw me?) Mother, wife –
everything flowed backwards, she was adrift – and daughter;
when had I slipped them, and she left shallow water?

Sundays

Such a delightful tableau –
I had been down to the pond with net
and wellingtons, jam-jar and pipette,
trawling the primal soup;
now, hunched at the dining-room table,
one eye glued to the microscope
I was having visions of the water-flea:
gasping for life, a teardrop, drowning, a heart beating wildly.

*

When I thread the bramble-grown grounds to see you,
no wife gently presses my arm, no children lag behind
to peer through cracked panes at abandoned wards . . .
When I sit by the scarred fishtank, frowning,
waiting for you to get your 'bits and pieces' together,
goldfish swarm to the side, as if I could free them;
ex-professor Sidney, dandyish in sky-blue cords
and trainers, mimics their blank pop-eyed look, his mouth
working soundlessly. We sit hours, hand
in clammy hand, the speech-bubbles going up between us;
you pat your hair, fiddle with a hem
and, staring round you wildly, fuss
about my precious time, the awful weather –
then look at me as if I could free you.

*

Back home, drinking, I switch on, and this aquarium teems
with phosphorescence, a perfect picture of the Id.
Children, join us on the good ship Venus!
Here is the blind albino crayfish,
the creature from the black lagoon; the raffish,
phallic flare-up of a cruising squid.

The Night Watch

Eight Bells

Night after night, I told you (though you couldn't hear)
that you'd soon be going home, and that, at home,
a large scotch was waiting. As I left intensive care
I'd take some comfort in that, some . . .

This one night I walked into the ward
I was more than a little surprised to see you sitting up,
smiling – you who'd so nearly gone for a burton;
tubes and needles, white and silver dial-studded box
rolled offstage behind a curtain.
Words seemed called for, but I couldn't find the word.
Strange, isn't it? you ventured. *To think that yesterday . . .*
You told me how they'd tried out one last drug – *Scotch!* –
and how, against the odds, *It seems it works.*
I hope your mother's kept that whisky waiting. Knowing her,
and you, I won't expect to find it half as easily
as this half-bottle, look, they've left in my drawer . . .

I was still trying to take all this in
when the telephone woke me. I thought my heart would stop
but it was yours that had given up the unequal struggle
some twelve minutes earlier. I checked my watch:
3.33. How many hours too soon? Had they guessed
what had started off the last attack? Found the tot-sized flask
I brought and watched you nip from (*Down the hatch*)
that last evening (though neither of us knew it then)
you'd spend awake, and able to speak? – Not much to ask,
but I can't remember your last words: *All the best*,
perhaps, or *Thanks for the scotch. We drinking men . . .*

Berths

Could anyone, we used to say, have wished you this?
A whole month, you were patient beyond belief
while new collapses came, and the ventilator's kiss,
a sucking drawn-out whisper, drowned out grief.

You'd have drowned without it, and without the drips
that left wounds in your neck, your side and wrist,
you'd have withered. You tried to come to grips
with them one night, but your weak hands missed
and pawed the air . . . I see you now on your last bed,
both you and it as cold and hard as stone,
you a stone lighter every day; each purplish clot
and bruise, the damp wisps on your forehead,
your eyes that looked as distant and alone
as the time you'd woken suddenly on a canvas fold-up cot,
a makeshift berth on an old friend's boat, looked out and
                                                                              seen
desert dawn-light, somewhere near El Alamein,
and felt the chafe of army-issue blankets on your skin –
a confused, sick fear took hold of you,
convinced for a second it was 1942,
convinced you had to live it all again.

I hardly wanted you to wake up, to scare yourself.
You've found your last berth, now, on my bedside shelf.

The Night Watch

Book of the film we watched five times
and knew by heart, *The Cruel Sea*
(abridged edition); *Small Craft on the Thames:
a Navigator's Guide*; *Mr. Midshipman Easy* . . .

In the watches of the night these gave him,
year in year out, a tolerable berth.
I played *Sink the Bismarck* in the bath
while he read *In Hazard* and *Lord Jim*

or razor-trimmed the tiny balsa blocks
for his model clipper-ships.
There were two cloth-bound, tattered books
from which he took his modelling tips:

'Varnish blocks-and-tackle, masts,
gunwhales, deck-structures, deck;
brasswork should be polished.' (In dry dock
on the mantelpiece – the horizon mists –

or riding at anchor on the chest-of-drawers
they're still as exact and beautiful.)
His sea-chest was long gone. And when his chest was
gone too, week in week out, dutiful

and faintly uneasy, I lugged
a new armful to his locker; he logged
up *Night-Watches* ('the Wapping wharves!'), Joshua Slocum,
Sailing Alone Around the World; *New Chum*.

My long night watches. I sat yawning
while he lay, nose, lungs bleeding.
Would it be *The Bird of Dawning*
or ('those sailing scenes!') *Dead Man Leading*?

Player's Navy

Brushing varnish on to brand-new window-frames,
sanding edges when the soiled, soaked rag
snags on splinters, I smell the shavings, bright wood
and the shining decks of twelve, thirteen; my head swims
with varnish, white spirit, timber-smells,
the oil of winches and of oiled wire rope. I tell myself
that this is what he would have wanted –
straightening up to light another Player's Navy Cut,
smoothing his moustache-ends with the back of his hand.
A passage from the River Plate – I signed up
for Southampton, second mate on the tramp steamer Capella;
at the Cape Verde Islands where we put in for coal
Silva came aboard (we called him Long John), selling
perfumes, knick-knacks, and was paid in Sunlight soap. . .

I tell myself that at last we were friends
as I reel back aboard after drinking in the Ship,
make the window-latches fast, batten down the hatches
of my skylights, lie down in the reek
of the years that I want back as the wind tugs harder
and listen to the room creak and strain at its moorings.

Keep-Net

We are fishing again, the Thames at Teddington, the two
of us have cycled here to set up canvas stools
on the towpath, and are fishing, some six feet apart,
slightly less than the length of my boyish greenheart rod,
that one day I shall watch disappear into the water
behind a careless canoe, that now bends lightly
as I reel in, and all the past swings lightly
into view, I reel it in, there with the float, the shot,
the shreds of bright green weed, the half-drowned maggot;
I prise the hook out of its mouth and it flashes briefly silver
in the keep-net, but has left a slime of scales on my hand,
there are scenes encoded there, messages I cannot read,
I am a child who mouths Our Father, in my books
Father Thames and Father Time are men with beards, like
                                                                    God;

my father has no beard, but a moustache he once shaved off
and only once, my mother made a fuss till it grew back;
he lights his Imperial Bruyere and it hangs lightly
from his mouth, the bright leaves flicker and I see through
grey-brown water his face coming nearer, bristly, smelling
of pipe-smoke; a pile of drawings, a photograph-enlarger,
swords and pictures on the walls, a dripping tap;
he runs across the lawn in his dressing-gown, maroon
spotted white, and waves his hands to shoo away our cat
that is mauling my ankle, my screams dying into sobs,
his dressing-gown billowing; he holds my head above water
as he tries to make me swim. The float bobs, I want him
to catch one too, more than I want to catch them all
myself, I who have caught the past, which is made of him,
maroon or silver flashes in a grey-brown river, into which I
                                                                    dive

as my rod, in slow motion, disappears, as the spools
of our reels click and whirr, click and whirr,
the Imperial Bruyere has fallen into my lap
as I wake, a book for keep-net, and mouth *My father*.

Cornish

The last message to come in
was a rumour bounced between stars
of fences down on an inland farm,
and a girl carrying a lamp upstairs
had seen a light far out, too far,
winking back in answer.

Next morning, it was gone.
But not a breath of breeze would stir
the mild, salt-haunted air,
or flutter the handkerchiefs held up by women
who came out slowly in the stupid calm,
each with a tiny flag drooping from one arm –
uncertain if they'd won
or what, if anything, they had to surrender.

Log

'The maelstrom! Could a more dreadful word in a more dreadful
situation have sounded in our ears! . . . From every point of the
horizon enormous waves were meeting, forming a gulf justly called
"The Navel of the Ocean", whose power of attraction extends to a
distance of twelve miles. There, not only vessels, but whales are
sacrificed, as well as white bears from the northern regions.'
                    – Jules Verne, *Twenty Thousand Leagues Under the Sea*

Myself, Fairford and the boy, deck-hands on the *Scarface*
(A. G. Pym, Tokyo-Nantucket) were huddled by Buxton,
                              who took the wheel,
and Captain George Currie – when Jenkins, gnawing a
                                      frost-bitten sole,
turns to us his fat white moustache of frost and ice,
fluffy-looking, like a kid all stuck with candy-floss
or ice-cream from a cornet – but with something of his Dad's
who was in whalers before him (*his* Dad remembered
                              the days of sail).
At first he'd laughed, called it *the rime of the ancient mariners*,
but now he turned with a glint in his eye, shouted *Steady lads!*
This here's the maelstrom, the navel of the ocean!
– sort of barmy voice. We thought he'd begun to rave
but looked out, scraping white stars from the ports of the
                                              deckhouse
and saw, miles around, from every point of the horizon,
running towards the gulf, enormous wave on wave . . .

It was weeks since we'd lost sight of the fleet – seen only
                                        pack-ice
drifting farther and farther south, and not a single whale,
not a single living thing, neither sea-bird nor seal;
then yesterday, early morning watch, Soutar cried out twice –

Fuckin' Christ man there's bears on it, and peering under the
                                                             fleece
of our hoods we could see them moving, outlines, shadows,
white on whiter white; and terror stabbed each soul
at how long we'd been steaming north. We stood like
                                                    mourners
as Cladd ran for'ard, fired; watched the spirit that was
                                                    Cladd's
explode out of him in a white cloud, a frosty exhalation.
Chedglow chipped him off of the gun with an ice-pick;
we boiled and ate most of him, stewed with scurvy-cress,
stowed the leftovers, the dainties, which were instantly frozen.
Last night I dreamt of dressed fingers, toes in aspic,

and today we saw the bear we'd skewered – one more
                                                    sacrifice,
crumpled, wasted . . . A moment later we hit the swell,
white swirls, foam plunging, *each wave swallowin' itsel'*,
Soutar screamed, and we were drawn in, down, but not to a
                                                    green-white peace –
for there alongside us, as we sank further from the floes,
swam a multitude of dead or dying things: otters, gulls, their
                                                    eyelids
clogged shut, fur and feathers claggy with effluents, oil;
among the whaling-boats, trawlers, ketches, catamarans
we saw blood-spattered seals, tunny trailing swim-bladders;
whales spilling pink froth, each stuck like a huge pin-cushion
with harpoons; pocked, distended creatures, as from a
                                                    blasted ark –
all this Jenkins begged me to set down, not to secure for us
pardon, still less Larsen's fame, but so that we might keep
                                                    our reason
should we come back alive out of this deep cold, this dark.

Free Enterprise

He has sat out many a pogrom
working on a new high-profile programme.
His interests are tied up
with information, an end

in itself. He owns other people's futures
and the hardware that kills.
He owns the radar-scanner
and the satellite-dish,

he owns your every word and wish.
He owns the wounds and the sutures.
He owns the works and the spanner.
He owns the skills.

He has kept only the friend
who will never outreach him,
and after a hard day at the interface
he summons to the screen

the latest play-pet, Trace
or Trudi or Teen.
A penthouse in Rotherhithe,
the rotors cutting like a scythe

through local custom, a wad
of petro-dollars, the air
above the heli-pad.
His pad is hell,

a shuttered shithole
full of expensive artworks.
The jacuzzi is a joke –
a platinum tapedeck –

but she's in it up to her neck
and he's at her dirtbox
with something as thick as a fist . . .
slap and trickle. Flick of the wrist.

She feels like she's going to die
or like she's already dead,
like the time he stopped the car
on the way up to Birmingham,

took her head
between his hands in the crowded lay-by
and made her gorge herself, *his star*,
at his open fly.

*

A rubber-baron, he grows fat on wives.
Almost every night, he listens
to the ghosts of money on his desk,
talking to him from the flickering screens.

He never sleeps. From dawn till dusk
he goes about his business, which is
to eat up more and more – more of the air,
more of the city's paving-stones and mud,

more flesh and blood,
and turn them into shit; he will spend,
enormously, to this end
the money he has married. *Bitches*.

Lunchtimes, in his favourite restaurant
his greed goes out in great waves.
He watches something bleed onto his plate
and blebs of fat coagulate.

His heart. His waistline. Sweat glistens
on his forehead. He must take more care.
So, after brandies, to the sauna, the gym –
he will groaningly prepare

to do unto others
before they do it unto him.
Then to Shepherd Market
and rubber-suited Cindy. *I shall/shall not want*

a chauffeur/pilot/P.A./companion
to be placed at my disposal throughout the conference.
He'll take Cindy, drop her at her mother's . . .
The Contessa has gone out somewhere

(she always has), an opening
(he settles with the mail
and a chunky tumbler-full of scotch), a private view.
Bills. Statements. Invitations. Sales

of the family condoms show a marked
increase: the epidemic is good news
(and even – how he hated it – the odd *boff*
de politesse is definitely off).

It is time for his toys, his pastimes –
the video he picked up in New York
with a female lead whose début was posthumous,
a platinum coke-spoon, a gold watch that can talk.

*

A rich silt
all the way from Zeebrugge
slides across the Astrakhan rugs
in the home of Sir Staunchly Sterling.

He sits late, he has reports to prepare.
Those who refuse to share
in the benefits of progress . . .
will learn that time . . . that time . . .

He does not see the stain,
greyish, thick
as an oil-slick,
easing its way towards him.

But when sleep finally comes swirling
like black air, stiff with salt
and the smell of diesel,
through his brain,

the white knobs of drowned skulls
bob up the stairs and crowd each room
in the home of Sir Staunchly Sterling.

Pornography

'Neither Cedar of Lebanon,
nor the dome
of St Paul's,
nor the round heart
of the cemetery, can be seen
from Highgate Hill;
rich Julius Beer
so loathed the world,
would so condemn
his fellow-men,
he built here
his huge monument –
thus shutting off
such sights from them
for ever. His wife
and women-folk
consume him for ever now
in the public places of Hell,
brandish on a fork
his head, and a Bill
of Rights for cannibals.'
– Grey, mid-winter
light, tangled evergreens;
vaults and sepulchres,
all broken,
crumbling, all overgrown . . .
Silent, we wait
for the sermon on the mount
to continue,
and see – unfurled
among bracken,
holly, ivy, ferns
(wreaths, gone to seed,
flourish on what's inside
the rotting dead),
angels fallen from grace

and shattered urns –
a woman, spread
unnaturally wide,
her flesh stark white
against the black mulch
of earth, of paths
that cover
common graves,
and, black
against it,
thick sprawling thatch;
she leans back
with a full-lipped grin.
You recoil
from the torn
glossy page
and from my thin,
foolish laugh –
you recoil with rage
but she, too, or rather
what was done to her
on this spot
by someone who left
a trail of
cuckoo-spit
on the purplish cleft
or across her face –
she, too, as much
as bramble, thorn
and nettle in
impenetrable groves,
is a part of life
in this deathly place . . .
The voice drones on:
our Virgil among
the illustrious
Victorian shades
is open-necked, young,

wears steel-rimmed specs,
has dandruff, a boil,
his mind on sex –
he is telling us
how Dante
Gabriel Rossetti
could not get over
hearing how
his young wife's hair
had gone on growing
in her tomb,
how men saw it glowing
like a glory
by the light
of their bonfire
on the night
they worked to exhume
poems buried with her
as he refused to be –
death-in-life, and art,
and corpse-colonnades
of wealth and fear!

L'Esprit de l'escalier

'My room is three and a quarter miles from here, but I must go to bed as there is a rhinoceros over the mantelpiece.' (Peter Fleming)

I had to be picked up and driven down,
of course. In the car three strangers – though not,
naturally enough, to each other – ignored you-know-who
while they recalled weekends in earlier days, a hunt,
a shoot, some legendary do.

It was all hilarious: what Jamie did
when he found them on the billiards table, what Toby said
when Jock jumped ship and nose-dived straight into the quay,
but I couldn't force myself to laugh along with them;
I was a prig, a spoil-sport – *me*,

the spare man, mystery guest, backstairs boy.
When I found my dinner-jacket laid out on the bed,
my shirt and trousers pressed, I wanted this to happen all
the time
and wondered if I had *l'esprit de l'escalier*
(I thought it meant the wit to climb).

I took an interest in the period and style –
names like *Inigo* and *Capability* began to mean a lot.
How could I say, When I last saw anywhere like this
it was on an outing with my mum and dad – we paid?
Beeches, elms in immemorial stasis . . .

And the rooms! I took a bath in one
that was bigger than my London flat. The maid came in,
fiddled with the sash and was almost out again
before she saw me. I whipped on my flannel fig-leaf
and, with a little swish, she was gone.

I'd never given much thought to conversation;
now here I was, simpering for my supper. Was it on
to be the bookish type? No, there was always someone else
who'd read more than I had, who'd published, in fact,
three 'really rather good' novels.

I lacked agility *and* confidence – *bons mots*
were beyond me, I never knew who was being talked about.
That left the lovable bohemian, a reprobate, a rake,
charming, *ingénu* (I once rose when the women did);
definitely gifted; on the make.

Why did the daughters always want it from behind –
was it the childhoods of dogs and horses? Why did they say,
Fuck me, harder, oh God, fuck me when I came, as if on cue?
One slipped back to one's room at dawn, before Maisie arrived
with tea. But Maisie always knew . . .

I had to be driven back. The morning walks,
the games of patience or charades, the old girls and boys
with beautiful manners; the room where Evelyn Waugh
started *Scoop*. The chapel where I prayed for the patience
to love. To stop being a bore.

The London Dissector

Art Lovers

She wants to see Hyde Park, Trafalgar Square, the Tower.
Instead, in the Tate you lecture her for an hour
on Bacon's rawness, his grasp of Renaissance Rome,
of *the things that happen with two people in a room* . . .
(Almost all, these days, best forgotten. To forget,
you walk the streets, or drink; but streets bring back
the rooms things happened in, or might have, you forget –
an attic in Holland Park, a basement in Hackney. Back
to square one, the room above a shrub-lined square
in Pimlico, or was it Primrose Hill? She lay in black
bra and slip, still, not sleeping. – It's quite a scare;
so you try drinking. On the way to the pub, willows
through sunlit drifts of smoke weep their reflections
into water. – She buried her face in the pillows.
And important suddenly, her foreign inflections,
her stillness, her weeping. Do you get the picture yet?)

Rhymers

It's called the *Cheshire Cheese*, but it's a *chop-house*,
you repeat and explain between mouthfuls; not a
                                                    cheese-shop.
A chop bleeds on your plate, and blood, in little eddies,
                                                    swirls
towards the middle. Your soul, which *low culture has*
                                                    nourished,
feels at home here (though *you are too many*, though
it's Fleet Street – not the place *where Dr Johnson flourished*
but where everything screams *Failure* at you . . .)
Was it in Borough you shared a mattress with two girls?
Lane after narrow lane, familiar – *Ma chère.* –
She's staying in one of the murky streets near Guy's.
You have a drink and start on *resurrection-men*
and the *London Dissector*; read out the bit where he dies
coughing bright red, like your dear dead daddy; chain-

smoke, blub. You gape at a pair of red pants
draped – *a red rag to a bull, or danger* – on the chair
to dry, and this is the drooping soul of romance . . .

Marvellous Boys

The packetboat is full of honeymooning couples
headed for your city of light; *how it gladdens us,*
you say, *to be travelling against the stream,*
makes us serious and strange to each other.
You chuff towards a cathedral filled with steam,
the current bears you on to a lodging-house
in Camden Town (the landlady scares you more than Arthur),
French conversation lessons, fucking, quarrels, pubs.
You wake to the noise of all the churches in St Pancras –
les voix d'enfants, chantant dans la coupole –
and would like to blow them sky-high. In a room full of
                                                    mummies
at the heart of the tomb called the British Museum
you see a left foot that a rat has nibbled
and shiver: Africa. On the bus, punk-rockers,
parodies of *him*: spike hair, a safety-pin through a nipple,
a girl with shaved head and (she shows you) green pubes.

Whitechapel

She tried on an old dress of her mother's; you wrote
(this was in your *First Love* phase), It's strange,
the way they dress each other for the sacrifice.
But now you name names, theories, candidates who range
from lunatics to royalty; Gull, your favourite . . .
You want to trace each doorway, entry and courtyard
where one of 'five unfortunates' was drawn and quartered,
the final, blood-flecked, sweating room, the festoons
he hung around it, made of her intestines,
the banner of meat, bleeding; the ruined face
and always the stark white body spread on grey
mattress-ticking, on a narrow bed of stains . . .
She is open, vulnerable; you drag up the soaked stones

of Smithfield, *meat-cathedral*, running full-tilt into an aisle
of grinning heads (why do you dabble in this?); your sickly smile,
she's scared, she wants – better you went home, you agree.

Nineties

Remember nights you breezed in to the Café Royal
for gins and absinthes with the poetry crowd,
poured wine and *bons mots* down Lydias and Giselles?
Then tottered back, weeks later, muzzy, to your rooms
through a Nocturne by Whistler, turned up wicks on lamps
and penned a few impressions in tetrameter, with rhymes?
(You favoured ABBA.) The girls were all gazelles;
London was a gaslit heaven, a *flower that, at last
like Dante's rose, opens to the moonlight, soft
as a yielding breast when whalebone is unlaced* –
Good, that. Morning, and the pile of envelopes and stamps,
a hock-and-seltzer, then: *My dear Symons/Dowson/Gosse* . . .
(They're all dead, stupid: gone where everyone goes,
the scribblers and the muses, ash in a slow sift.
Who writes letters now? Get down the Cow & Crud
with Mick and Kevin, for a pint of something *real*.)

Late Show

You go to Lauren's place – she makes Bucks Fizz,
you snort a line or two – and then it's out for eats,
your usual, the Romantica, where everyone *knows*.
But something's wrong. The single long-stemmed rose
you sent a week ago stares back from the primitive vase;
its long stem has become the shortest fuse.
When you were postgrads (Lauren's 19th-century lit.,
M.A. Harvard) you shared a kitchen, *just like Keats
and Fanny* (shy looks when you met in the hall);
she was always there to go to from the bluestocking drawl . . .
Now it's black sheets, a penthouse view of blazing blocks,
of masts and rigging in a hundred dry historic docks.
Does she think, *Will he ever learn where to find my clit*
or does she think (you do) you're boyish, witty, wise?

She's fuelled up for one of your more memorable rows.
Petal by petal, silently, you eat the rose.

Poésie de départs

Five minutes from your flat, alongside the canal,
a pub where you're not known. Trees are skeletons round here
but sunlight butters up the stucco, ignites houseboats, canal
(what was it you couldn't say?). You sip your beer
and think of her (she couldn't sleep); then you walk on –
the slant of rippling light on bricks, on moss and ferns
under bridges, is enough to bring you to your knees
(*O la rivière dans la rue*); another pub, another beer.
There was that freckled back and shoulder-blade somewhere –
Blackheath, Bloomsbury? And some nights were Camberwell's –
Camberwell was white skin, soft skin, pitch-black hair.
You sit a while and drink, frown at the *canaille*,
drowned in dreams and burning to be gone –
watch them as they go, that one holds a furnace
in her walk – then come back to these four white walls
to look for lost connections on your hands and knees.

Toilette

It might be that small cottage
off Ship Street,
where any man would lead you up the garden path.

It might be, for convenience,
anywhere in Brighton, Bath,
Charing Cross, Soho, Notting Hill.

It's like something from *The American Friend*,
a numbness starting at your feet,
someone stirring your mess of pottage
and taking you apart.

·The blade that brings a last flush
spreading from your still-
warm heart.

The knives put back carefully, end
to end – that sly hint of deviance;
your trying not to blush.

Mohican

Nothing, nowhere, he was tiny,
playing soldiers in the backyard,
when his salesman father sent him
picture-postcards – London, England:
Big Ben, Hampton Court, the Hilton.
Later on his father left them,
mother, son; she hit the bottle,
he dropped out and started drifting –
classic story. But the upshot? –
He had never learned discretion
is the better part of valour,
heard a war was there for winning,
and enlisted as a soldier . . .
Now he lives in London, England,
working as a barman, bouncer,
heavy, in a club in Soho;
works out daily, builds his body
to a hard and handsome weapon,
shaves his skull in a Mohican,
stripe of hair left down the middle –
frightens even his employers,
but they like that; he is black belt,
martial arts, can kick like Bruce Lee,
kill a man with just two fingers.
Outwardly, though, he is gentle,
buys rice-wine and veg for stir-fry
at the Chinese supermarket;
daytimes, in the park, does Tai-chi,
graceful, limpid; has read *Zen and*
(weird) *the Art of Motorcycle*
Maintenance, also *Despatches*;
watches in a daze those movies –
Taxi Driver, some new westerns –
where the white man is the loser.
Here he is in tracksuit, trainers,
riding on the London subway –

so why *is* he staring, wide-eyed,
trembling, sweating, at the Asian
student opposite, who fidgets,
full of unease, turns to whisper
to her friend – both young, both lovely,
T-shirts printed *Save the Forest* –
in a tongue he recognises?

*

*'The first time the Americans came
they gave the children sweets to eat –
we didn't know their language, but they said* Okay,
and so we learnt that word, Okay.

*The second time, we gave them water to drink.
They didn't say anything, that time.*

The third time, they killed everybody.'

'I saw a lot of bodies in a ditch, it upset me.'

*'My sister was fourteen that year. I looked out
of the house and saw an American pressing on
top of her. She had no clothes on. She was trying
to resist him, but he went on pressing on her.
I didn't know then what that meant. When he had finished,
he got up, pulled his clothes up, and shot her.'*

Alarm

I was shaken at four
not by a footstep,
not by sirens in the street
and not by a scream
from the flat next door,
or a curt knock
at my own door,
but by my dream,
which drenched the sheet
and woke me to stare
at the glowing face
of a digital alarm-clock
that was one more scare,
that would not stop
its silly, silent farce
of adding number to number,
patiently, mindlessly
totting up the score
in a sort of game
that I couldn't remember,
till the meaning was clear
of both the dream and this,
this new-smelling fear,
and nothing would be the same
as I'd hoped or wanted,
and I had to bring back,
name by lost name,
each word, caress or kiss
expended on me
since the whole thing began:
so many hours, lost hours,
lost on sofas, floors,
on piles of coats at parties,
on beds and lawns and beaches
under different stars,
struggling with panties,

skirts pulled up, on stairs,
on mattresses in cold rooms,
on the back seats of cars;
floozies, flowers,
salesgirls, Sloanes,
typists, teachers,
barristers, barmaids,
air-hostesses, air-heads,
princesses, P Rs,
managers, mums –
they all came back
from wherever they'd gone,
and I couldn't pass the buck
and couldn't escape
into booze, or another
woman's body, a shape
I knew, woman-smells,
eyes closing, moans;
they all had strange smiles,
and some were reproachful
and some apologetic,
but I couldn't tell who
had killed me, or whom
I had killed, or whether
I was hunter or hunted,
pimp or punter,
convicted man or screw;
or what I was to do
with each new coachful
of pain and anaesthetic,
Kleenex, pills, address-book,
too many vodkas, rums,
a torn dress, a broken shoe.

Safe

1

You'd already cancelled twice. *Third time rucky*,
old Chinese proverb; so – the Good New World, or
the Holy Fook? Your theme was *Down in old Hong Kong*,
mine was *I'm not asking to be understood* . . . The old new
song.

It was playing on your transistor in the morning
but ours was the silence of the almost-ashamed,
too old for shyness and yet far from ease.
The night before, you'd slipped into something more
comfortable

and I'd watched you fall apart as I parted your knees –
now it lay chalk-smeared and crumpled, flung on the floor
while you took your shower; and I shammed
a cool unconcern, as if this was nothing new,

nothing at all, since that was what you wanted me to do.
You dressed, went out, spent half the day star-fucking
and the rest biting the heads off snakes –
these and other quick snacks.

2

Fifteen years since our *ménage
à cinq ou six*, you call from all the way
across the world, a condo in Oregon, to say
How come we're still friends? It's strange –

and now, to please myself, I recall the faded
red and blue flowers on your kimono, a still-flagrant
hand-me-down from your mother, an exotic bloom
among the teenage junk and jumble of my room;

recall, too, the other rooms in which it flared;
the stiff white sheets on a bed in a room in Florence,
its tiled floor, its black furniture, the long slow fuck
we had there, hardly believing our luck;

a shuttered room in Sestri that was never aired;
a room in Fécamp where the bed was never made;
our last room, a hot-house basement in Blackrock.
You said, *Do it now, while I'm holding your cock.*

3
They are all there to be fucked. There is not one
who has not been fucked every way under the sun
by long or short, thick or thin, soft or hard,
bald-as-an-egg or all-over-wiry-haired.

They smile familiarly, though, as if they saw
love looking on them, the eye of something more:
and this one, stretched naked on a wicker *chaise*,
fourteen or fifteen – she knows what men are like, and do,

                                her gaze

is bold and shy, hurt and aloof . . .
Storyville, 1912, his contraptions come to life
with a soft explosion, his huge domed head makes a rearing
                                     hummock
under a sheet, his eye swivels to her blurry stomach –

men, years, have pocked and stained the plate
I press my mouth to, against the grain; on my palate
the sharp taste of her life, her death, what happened to her,
on my tongue the word *savanna*.

Greenheart

We came on them stretched out in a clearing,
feet and hands hacked off, privates in their mouths;
the gaudy shrieks beyond their blood-blocked hearing
with the echoes of their screams, the shots' aftermath –
I'd heard the loud black apparatus rise
and flap back, like the beating of giant moths
and bats that filled the ballroom with their cries
when Harry shouldered his way into a decade's
shuttered darkness at the Hotel de la Cruz –
the clapping hung, like flies on half-decayed
faces, in the still, hot blur of trees,
in thick green folds of forest . . . Then *OK, dickheads,*
keep your hands where I can see them. Freeze!
– the tone of the P.E. master's loutish sneer –
came from behind us, and in twos and threes
they loped from the bush, each a human snare
that bristled with knife, machete, automatic weapon;
jungle rig, stubble-shadowed face, a smear
of mud or blood on the cheekbones, sort of warpaint;
red-eyed, blank looks. I was sure we'd had it
there and then, but the tallish leader, wiping
sweat from his forehead, skull – he was shaven-headed
under the green képi – studied us in turn
through narrowed eyes; grim-mouthed, grave, he nodded
to the others, made a new sound (stern
but less sadistic than resigned), and trekked
with the slackly slouching gait of a Soho slattern
towards the thicket, the overgrown green track
out of that killing-ground. I was to follow,
I gathered from the goading of the gun at my back,
and so were Hugh and Harry; but Hugh, poor fellow,
whipped round with a reflex of anger – stupid, brave,
say what you like, both of them sound hollow –
and jabbed at his tormentor. Curses, brief
and terrible, rang out; a machete flashed, bright, cold;
Hugh's lean young body, come to grief,

fell forward, spurting blood; twitched and lolled;
and bouncing once, like a coconut at a fête,
mouth working soundlessly, his blond head rolled
in its own red carpet to my feet.

Permission to bury him was curtly refused.
After four days' hard going in the bush
we came to a stockade – not knowing what we faced:
gun-emplacements, dogs; the plunge and thresh
of helicopters; acrid smoke from fires;
shouting men. *Looks like a frantic bish*,
said Harry, grinning, but I saw his worst fears
stand out like fever on his drawn white face.
We staggered on, past Indians building pyres
and heaping corpses on them – it seemed the place
had come under attack – then we were shoved
into a sort of shooting-lodge-cum-palace,
a well-appointed bungalow. We shaved,
showered and shat, and were summoned to a room
in which a careful harmony had been achieved
between the hunting-trophies and the views of Rome,
the birds in cages, flecks of glazed green fire,
and the rings on the fingers of the man on the sofa drinking rum.
One of his hands abstractedly kneaded the fur
at the neck of a chained leopard – though its chain
looked endless, it looped, in fact, as far
as a sticky mound of red meat (that had been Chan,
a Chinese associate, we were later told)
in the yard, and back to rest beneath the chin
of our host, to tangle with his chest-hair. 'Gold,
gentlemen' (he noticed that my eyes
had lit on it), 'like much I own, solid gold.
I'm sure you're curious as to how – otherwise
you would not be here – how I came by . . . *all this*.'
(He gestured vaguely.) 'I could tell how it was
in the beginning, the streets, the gangs, the genesis
of the killer in the college-kid – but, shit, man,
what would you make of it? A piece of piss

like you . . . Kicks and money're all of it, man,
I just loved the work. Once you've cut one throat
you can cut another, you're a hit-man.
They saw me, they knew they were under threat.
Contract stuff. *Not murder, but a sacrifice* –
who said that? Some poet . . . I put them through it.
But the big deal was cocaine, the rich man's vice.
For a while, I smuggled emeralds as a front –
a front! White gold. Emeralds. Snow. Green ice.
Hollywood, New York, a million suckers on the hunt
for the big blow, happy trails – I've seen grown men
so high, they were packing some chick's cunt
with coke, and eating it right out again.
She weren't complaining . . . Like business, I got big,
built some factories, airstrips, this place – then
I trained an army, bought a local bigwig
(I blew away the ones I couldn't buy)
and settled in. I mean to stay. And when some pig
from another set-up, when the CIA, FBI
or DEA want to waste me, like
they tried at dawn today – well, they'll die
but not too quickly: out back there's a lake
full of alligators, and you've met Ramón,
my colonel with the Yul Brynner look
(he gets a kick from feeding pussy on
the bodies he can cut up still alive
and panting to be let go, until they're gone.)
Sure, I've got some problems right now, I've
got the military sitting on my tail
and though I've spent enough to earn the people's love
some still prefer the Marxist's way of toil –
guerrillas (that's *gorillas*) in the hills –
would you believe some mercenary, some big tool
from London, England, thought he'd pay his bills
by picking up a contract on me? *Shit!*
Soon I'll have kids, out of their heads on crack or pills
I've sold them, coming here to make a hit . . .'

That evening, over dinner – some rich stew
of fish and fowl (for, though we had not seen
the grey-brown, sepia river, it was nearby, we knew)
and the fruits of that breeding fume of green,
the bush; and manioc; and beer and bitter coffee –
I agreed, though with an inward groan,
to tell how we had come out here, all three,
in search of something; how an item in the *Times*
had mentioned Harry's father, a missionary
who vanished without trace in troubled times
while trying to spread the gospel of the one true faith
at a trading-post on the Xingu (teams
of anthropologists, explorers, men of pluck and pith
had failed to find him, failed to bring back word);
how Hugh, prizewinning author of *The Shining Path*:
Peru at the Crossroads, specialist reporter, heard
that crack-downs in Colombia, cartels at war
meant all the old distinctions were now blurred
and, commissioned by *Time-Life* (one-off, he swore)
and the *Observer*, hopped on the next plane;
how, listening one Christmas to my mother's endless store
of reminiscence, I had idly formed a plan
to make my way from Somerset to Guyana
and find my uncle's old greenheart plantation,
abandoned when the *British* went out of *Guiana*;
how, finally, before we had pulled back, as
each one would, the curtain of lianas,
creepers, wrecked vines, tendrils, leaves – our trackers,
bearers, guides looking fathomlessly on –
we had met up at the Country Club in Caracas
and dined with Reading, ex-consul, ex-con,
old colonial hand and classicist,
poet, small-hours philosopher who when far gone
in drink, as he most often was, would insist
on holding forth in loud hexameters;
how he told us in this way (though pissed)
that we might find (his utterance, always terse,
bordered on the cryptic here) *what all men seek*

somewhere up-country, a place, *though none of it matters*
except at a purely personal level, that men forsake,
where birds cry out in pain, and nature suffers a curse.
'So we joined forces, bade farewell to that old soak
and came, weeks later, to the Hotel de la Cruz.'

At this our host's eyes widened. 'And, you found? . . .'
'Nothing', I went on, 'but an empty shell,
a building sinking back into the ground,
reclaimed by jungle, the husk of an hotel.'
'That's all?' 'Except that, in an upstairs room,
when Hugh broke down the door, a voice croaked *Well.*
You're here at last. We peered into the gloom
and saw a man cross-legged on a bed,
caked in bat-shit; then he seemed to loom
up, a skeleton with dark enormous head
and yards-long, thick white beard. *I knew you'd come.*
O'Hanlon's the name, this apparition said,
but call me Redsi. Have some peanuts. Rum?
He reached behind him, and – I promise you –
unplugged a bottle from his bony bum.
I gasped and turned and ran, and, shouting, Hugh
and Harry followed, half-falling over themselves.
And that was all we found there, but for bats, and two
huge wooden boxes, stacked on shelves
in the foul-smelling kitchen; and in these,
plump white plastic packets, pillows for elves.
All three of us round the boxes on our knees –
Hugh split one packet, sniffed and tasted. Sort of snuff,
I thought, and like snuff it made me sneeze.
Hugh, I noticed, put a packet of the stuff
in his rucksack when we left, alarmed by each
(*Off the tee*, said Harry, *and into the rough*)
shrill shriek and squawk and sudden screech,
the noise of tree-top colonies, the mechanical shout
of birds and insects in their meshed arcades, the creatures
of loud hot light and silent, cool damp shade;
we saw only trees and scrub, heard dense flocks fly up

whenever one of us stopped to take a shot:
unbroken walls of green, green waterfalls that flow up –'

'You had already entered my . . . kingdom', our host put in,
and I was silent. Helpless fury welled up, sank.
I looked at him, a great distorted grin.
'Most entertaining. Thank you. But who is it I thank?
My name is Silvano, *alias* Silva. You are . . . ?'
He extended his jewel-encrusted hand. 'Bowerbank,
Gavin Bowerbank. This is Harry Ormerod-Carr,
and our young friend, my cousin, so ruthlessly cut down,
was the Hon. Hugh Greenwood. I might go so far
as to challenge you to give me some redress at dawn
for his life, with weapons of your choice –' '*My choice*?!'
– 'if I did not know you for a bully and – since what's done
isn't even by your hand – a coward.' I'd raised my voice;
now I quietened once again. In a flash, Silvano,
who was sallow olive, turned a livid green; high voice
the more menacing for sounding *molto piano*,
he said, 'On the contrary, my friend, I'll meet you
to settle this in six hours' time. I'll . . .' (almost soprano)
'fight you with machetes, and I'll beat you.
I'm not some Indian or Ladino scum,
some piece of shit – I'll have Raoul cook and eat you
for what you've said; and, since it's clear we've come
to the end of talking, I'd like to let you know
just how deep you're mixed up in this jungle scam,
Mr Fuckin' Nose-in-Air, Mr Do-No-
Evil, Speak-No-Evil, Ass-in-Fuckin'-Hell.'
I reeled back, flabbergasted. '*Numero uno*,
you think it was so great for the guys your uncle
bought and sold? You think they loved him for the way
he took their land, their women and their lives? He'd sunk all
he had in greenheart, so he had to make it pay;
then inside two years he'd sunk all that in booze
and crazy expeditions, looking for *le pays
d'or*, Eldorado; found the Hotel de la Cruz
instead, shipped down the widows and the daughters of

the men he'd killed (the ones he couldn't use)
and started cashing in. The place was like a sieve:
full of holes, through which dirt and riches poured –
enough spunk was spilled in it to save
the human species from extinction (some were spared,
and brought up to their mothers' trade; some not).
He'd taken everything, and now he took their spirit
from the trees, the greenheart he left to rot.'

(Through all this Harry and myself sat, stunned,
astonished, almost stupefied.) With that he stood:
'Since you're my guests, I now invite you to get stoned,
just like the Preacher. You're surprised? That stud,
your uncle, did all he could to populate the place
but he had help – every little half-caste bastard
belonged to Unc, or else to his accomplice,
your daddy, Carr; well, you've all met him . . .'
This latest information seemed to nonplus
Harry, seemed, in fact, to find him not at home.
'The old man turned up there one day, the Hotel,
looking pretty bad, raving, *the Indians would get him*
if the flies and fever didn't, some half-ass tale
of how, at his one-horse mission not far from the coast
the people had begun to die – *A quiet hell,*
influenza, smallpox, these things are the cost
for them – those were his words – and when his crucifix
and prayers and Bible failed to save them, they had cursed
their new god and prepared to offer up a sacrifice –
him – to the old . . . But he escaped when Muldoon,
a defrocked priest who used to trade in sassafras,
heard of his trouble and strapped him to a mule . . .
At the Hotel he got his mind back – half of it, at least;
took three wives: *Left Leg, Right Leg, Middle One,*
and may the Spirit of the Rum be blest,
Cassiri and the Coca-leaf be blest – that was his creed –
O mulier multitudinis: man, he was a blast.
Life in that Hotel was . . . a little *crude*,
if you take my meaning; in time they all checked out,

your uncle Greenheart (he was called that by his crowd
of sex-slaves – he was hard, and, when he was chicked out,
crazy, but he could bend) along with the rest;
the Preacher hung on in there like a chigoe
when it gets under your skin. He rides the crest
of a cocaine-wave – the place is useful to me now –
and takes himself for some fool Jesus Christ
or some explorer my men killed. So what's new?'

He turned and left us. Neither of us spoke
as we were escorted to our sleeping quarters
(we declined salt-cellars of white snuff). A spark
from a match, some curt, unpleasant-sounding orders
and I was alone in darkness. I can't believe I slept
(imagine for yourself my state of mind), but from the borders
of sleep I started up as a shadowy figure slipped
inside the wire-meshed door (mosquitoes in a whining cloud,
the whirring fan); bare feet distinctly slapped
on concrete; I lay as if manacled,
cat's-eyes, an unfamiliar smell came through the air
and a woman loomed above me, scantily clad.
Her face curved down to mine, I felt her hair
fall around me like a curtain – and she whispered low:
'This may be your last chance. We'll be OK here,
they won't disturb us. What you don't already know
I'll teach you; and I'll do anything you want.'
She touched my cheek; took my hand, placed it below
the brown-blue blotch of a nipple. 'I'd r-rather you w-went',
I stammered as she moved it slowly down her stomach
until it touched – 'And what if I won't?' –
a firm, round, glistening, smooth hummock,
damp fuzz beneath that. I wiped my sweat-drenched eyes
with my other hand, tried to sit up in the hammock
(a mistake); she smiled, defiant, mischievous but wise
beyond her years, her taunting stare. 'I'll call the guard.'
'You idiot. First he'd fuck me, two, three ways,
then force you to fuck me too. You're getting hard' –
she put her hand on me – 'See? Call him, and watch

what happens, or better still, enjoy my gourd.'
She took her fingers off me – I could feel myself twitch –
and thrust them into her black tuft; rocked to and fro.
My eyes fixed on that jungle, 'Are you a witch?'
I asked. She laughed, a long laugh, deep and free.
'A witch? No, but I'm here to cast a spell.'
Her head dipped, warm wet engulfed me, I read *Ro-sa-de-Fon-se-ca* on her back . . . I was about to spill
but pulled away. 'I can't make you want this,'
she said; 'you're pretty weird. Silvano'll spoil
that face of yours, like he does' (now more a hiss
than human speech) 'with everything.' This was the voice
of experience, no doubt. 'But, for one kiss –
I'll help you get away from here.' Spawned in vice
and raised in it, schooled in Miami, Bogotá –
the fleshpots and perspiring tropic dives –
she was offering to save my life. I looked at her
and saw two doves fly up from their armpit-roosts;
her hidden folds and clefts now seemed to utter,
not a musky otto, but attar. 'My future rests,
Madam, not in your hands but in my own;
not on your favours, between your legs or breasts,
but in the strength and courage I have always shown
a world too heedless of itself to keep from harm.'
She bent close again, and I saw both eyes shine
like a tiger's, but with a kindly light; she raised her arm
and crossed the air above me; then she stooped
for a third and final time, and placed on my wrist a charm,
a bracelet she slid from the slim wrist it *had* looped.
'This will protect you when you face your enemies'
(a dreadful cry pierced the thin partition); tight-lipped,
I took it (a drawn-out sob). 'First, the enemas.
Then they'll have their fun with him – your friend Harry –
and then they'll have more fun, with him *and* me.
It all gets filmed. Please don't be in a hurry
to help him – you can't, no-one can.' She was gone.
I staggered, reeling, blinded, to a chink – the horror! –
Harry, two guards and the girl, one flesh; a gun

in Harry's mouth, Harry in hers . . . My pounding blood
kept time with the blows the guards began
to rain; a buzzing screech, a blade; everything was blood.

I must have fainted – when I next saw day
a huge paw was shaking me. One thought –
'This is the day on which I am to die' –
went through my mind, and shortly after that
I faced Silvano, spruce in his green fatigues,
both of us armed to the teeth, at
the appointed place and time. My own togs
were pretty well in tatters – I must have made
a sorry sight; I noticed he wore dog-tags
(though gold ones) in paramilitary mode,
and recalled the bracelet. Fired by that memory
I advanced on him, and died there in the mud –
though what transpired was this: stock-still, marmoreal
he offered his thick neck, his swart head;
I offed it in three swipes; his next bit of mummery
froze my blood and stopped my heart. For instead
of toppling, calmly he bent and picked up by the hair
his own head; holding it at arm's length, stood
upright; turned it on me – did I truly see and hear
these things? – and, as if it had been
a pumpkin-lantern (though it glowed with an eerie
greenish light, and dripped stuff that was *green*)
he was clutching, and the whole episode
no more than a foolish prank at Hallowe'en,
held his ground as the lips creaked open, said:

'What can you still stand to know? How fast the forest
is burning up, what cattle on the cattle-farms are forced
to eat – which you then eat, hamburger-head? First

the white men fucked the Indians, and we're still fucking
them.

Oh yes, they'll learn our principles of trade, in time.
It's not as if we've ever worked together as a team.

But one law behind all this, one lord of misrule;
one lord of the flies, of the virus (this is real),
of the flying fish and of us – instinctive, visceral;

you learnt it once, forgot it. Now learn that my name
will start you on the right track to the truth that I am –
more than rum or yoppo, that truth will make you numb.

Greenheart, Greenmantle, Greenaway, Harry, Hugh:
I'm all these, and Silvano; and Beelzebub too;
and Bertie Lake, bullion-robber on the run. And you.

You look amazed, and rightly. I'm not peddling *tapas*.
This trickster's games have tripped up jaguars and tapirs
and I traffic with the lives of tribes, of rubber-tappers.

Follow the trail back through the undergrowth, the trees,
through the prizes, record times and dazzling tries,
the rowing fours, the summer-evening centuries –

into something blacker than a black fruit's rind,
than a negro's skin, into the ramifying, overgrown
forest of yourself, into the rambling, ruined

hotel-rooms you call your mind, looped brilliance
and glooms, where you are constantly arraigned
for your desire to dominate, to keep your head, to hold your own.

Aged ten: *tingling with pride, hot with luck, you laid*
out, on a bed of cotton-wool, under a perspex lid,
a thrush you found flopped in a dusty corner
of the playground. It would be the star turn
on Parents' Night – Nature Club had the whole back wall!
Next day, you were smug, smiling all the way to school
but as you bounded into the classroom you felt small,
frightened; something had gone wrong. A nasty smell
thickened as you went nearer, made you retch –
and there, instead of the soft, plump, speckled swell
of its breast, maggots tumbled over themselves,
a grey mush. You whirled round, knocking jars off shelves;
pondweed, larvae and spawn spilled in a viscid pool

63

with tadpoles, water-boatmen, a terrapin at full stretch . . .
Eight: *heraldic, the stag-beetle never stood a chance*
in your kangaroo-court, nor the humble worm.
You yanked one's antlers out; chopped the other into bits
which you then pinned to the earth with nails
the better to watch them wriggle and squirm.
Their sufferings magnified you, little, afraid
of everything. You pulled apart two copulating snails,
intrigued by the white, capped member like a length of string,
then crunched them underfoot. You felt strong
as you broke off daddy-longlegs' long legs one by one,
tied a firework to a dog's tail and took bets
on how much it would leave, or trapped a spider you'd named Fred
under a magnifying glass and left them in the sun.

Make for Paradise Island, tell your tale and then keep silent.'